teach me about

Copyright © Joy Berry, 2022
Originally Published, 1986

All rights are reserved.

No part of this book can be duplicated or used without the prior written permission of the copyright owner, except for the use of brief quotations from the book.

For inquiries or permission requests contact the publisher.

Published by Joy Berry Enterprises
www.joyberryenterprises.com

teach me about

By JOY BERRY

Illustrated by Bartholomew

I like doing things.

I am happy when I am busy.

Sometimes it seems as if there is nothing to do.

I am not busy.

I am bored.

It is not fun to be bored.

I am not happy when I am bored.

I feel like whining.

I feel like throwing a tantrum.

Whining and throwing a tantrum do not make me happy.
They do not help me when I am bored.

I need to get busy

when I am bored.

I need to do something.

I do not want to get in trouble.

The things I do must be

all right with Mommy or Daddy.

I always ask before

I do something.

I do not want to get hurt.

The things I do must be safe.

I do not play with things

that could harm me.

I do not do anything

that could hurt me.

I do not want to break anything.

I am careful

with the things I play with.

There are many things I can do.

Sometimes I play with my toys.

Sometimes I do not want to play with my toys.

I find used things like boxes, bags, and plastic bottles that no one wants anymore.

I find old things around the house.

I ask if I may play with them.

I play with these things instead of with my toys.

Sometimes I want
to make something.
I use things like paper, crayons,
scissors, glue, or clay.
I make wonderful things.

Sometimes I want to play outside.

I crawl, run, jump, and climb.

At other times,

I play in the water, sand, or dirt.

I do not want to be bored

when I go away from home.

I take toys to play with.

I take books to look at.

I take things to do.

I do not leave a mess.

I pick up my toys.

I put my things away.

helpful hints for parents about
Boredom

Dear Parents:

The purpose of this book is
- to define boredom and its consequences, and
- to teach children how to entertain themselves with acceptable activities.

You can best implement the purpose of this book by
- reading it to your child, and
- reading the following *Helpful Hints* and using them whenever applicable.

STIMULATING ENVIRONMENTS

Here are some things you can do to make your baby's environment entertaining as well as educational:

General Decor
- Use bright, rather than pastel colors when decorating your baby's room. Red is a favorite color for most babies.
- Make patterns and moving objects a part of the decor in your baby's room.

Inside the Crib
- Use patterned sheets, blankets, and quilts.
- Attach a nonbreakable mirror to the side of the crib.
- Line the crib with simple, brightly colored pictures.
- Thread large paper clips on an elastic cord. Extend the cord across the bed. Tie it securely to both sides of the crib. Hang objects from the clips. Change the objects every few weeks.
- Put a see-through bumper pad in your baby's crib.

Outside the Crib
- Put cup hooks in the ceiling above the crib to hold mobiles. Hang the mobiles eight to twelve inches away from your baby's face. Change the mobile every few weeks.
- Use a hanger as a foundation for a mobile. Here are some items you can attach to the hanger:
  - colored paper
  - wrapping paper
  - tissue paper
  - cellophane
  - tinfoil
  - ribbon
  - yarn

- strips of cloth
- household objects (attached to the hanger with string, ribbon, yarn, or dental floss)
- Attach a lightweight, inflatable beach ball or an aluminum pie plate to a string, and tie it to the cup hook over your baby's crib.
- Hang a prism or crystals in the window.
- Hang brightly colored posters on the walls.

Play Spaces

Here are some things you can do to create an interesting play environment for your child.
- Allow your child to do messy activities in the shower or tub. Make sure there is a nonslip vinyl mat on the floor of the shower or tub.
- Use an inflatable swimming pool. This is also good for messy activities.
- Drape a sheet or blanket over a card table or chairs.
- Cut windows and a door out of an appliance box.
- Put up a tent.

TOYS

Safe Toys

The toys you allow your child to play with should be safe. Safe toys do not have

- sharp points
- sharp edges
- pinch points
- shear points
- springs or hinges
- cords over 12 inches long
- parts than can be swallowed

Safe toys are
- nonbreakable (too hard or too soft to break—no glass or brittle plastics!)
- nontoxic

- nonallergenic
- made of materials that can be cleaned and disinfected

Toy chests should also be safe. Remove the heavy lid or install a device which will keep the lid open on the toy chest.

Cleaning Toys

Keep your child's toys clean by doing one or more of the following:
- Have your child wash his/her toys during bath time.
- Have your child wash his/her toys with a hose outside.
- Put small toys in nylon net, drawstring bags. Put the bags of toys in the washing machine and wash them on the gentle cycle.
- Wash sturdy toys in the dishwasher using the gentle cycle.

Rotating Toys

- Keep your child interested in his/her toys by rotating them. Let your child play with some of the toys and put the others away. Rotate each toy at least once a month.

Simple Toys

Here is a list of items that can be used as toys:
- baseball cards
- cooking utensils
- a deck of cards
- egg cartons
- fuzzy tennis balls
- gift ribbons and bows
- a harmonica
- ice cube trays
- measuring cups and spoons
- napkin rings (to string)
- old magazines
- paper cups (to stack or nest)
- plastic containers, with and without lids
- pots and pans
- sponges, wet and dry
- textured fabric remnants
- toothbrushes

Here are some simple toys you can make:
- WAD. Loosely wad a sheet of cellophane, waxed paper, or wrapping paper.
- BRACELET. Tie ribbon loosely around your baby's wrist, or slip on a colored rubber band (one that does not fit too tightly).
- RATTLE. String large buttons, empty spools, or bells on a strong elastic cord.
- SHAKER. Fill an egg-shaped, pantyhose container (or any other plastic container) with sand, pebbles, corn, beans, rice, macaroni, bottle caps, washers, BBs, or bells. Seal the opening with strong glue. Then put tape over the seal.
- BOOK. Fill a photograph album with pictures from magazines.
- PICTURE PLATES. Paste magazine pictures to paper plates. Cover the picture and plate with clear contact paper.
- LACING. Knot a shoelace at one end. Give it to your child along with a colander. Show your child how to weave the shoelace in and out of the holes.
- SORTING. Use an egg carton and a variety of buttons. Let your child sort the buttons according to the color, size, and shape of the buttons. (This activity is for older children who will not put the buttons in their mouths.) Such things as dried macaroni, beans, and corn can also be used.

ACTIVITIES

Indoor Activities
- Provide a music box, tape recorder, record player, or radio for your child.

- Record "homemade" tapes featuring you or other relatives or friends, if your child has access to a tape recorder.
- Attach bells to your baby's booties. (Make sure they are securely attached.)
- Strap your baby into an infant seat. Put the seat on top of the washing machine during the spin cycle. Stay with your child until the experience is over.
- Place large pieces of colored tape on the crib sheet. Have your child remove the tape. (Be sure to take the tape away from your child immediately after it has been removed.)
- Make a textured walkway out of such things as doormats, bath mats, thick fabric samples, and carpet samples. Have your child walk or crawl along the walkway. Older children can make their own "textured sidewalks."
- Let your child wash nonbreakable dishes or a washable doll in the kitchen sink.
- Attach a variety of nonbreakable objects to the highchair with various lengths of elastic cord. Let your child throw the objects away and then retrieve them.
- Put your child in a walker and allow him/her to chase standing grocery bags or large wads of paper around the floor.

Outdoor Activities
- Put a trickling hose into an area with sand or dirt. Also provide large spoons, hand shovels, and containers.
- Let your child "paint" on the sidewalk or other surfaces with water and old paint brushes.

- Make a sandbox by filling a plastic wading pool with sand. Add a container of salt to the sand to discourage cats from littering the sandbox.
- Rub a dull slide with wax paper, or let your child slide down the slide on a sheet of wax paper.
- Cover the chains of a swing with sleeves made from old garden hose.

Miscellaneous Activities That Can Be Done Indoors or Outdoors

- Hide a surprise in a container for your child to find. The container can be a small brown bag, a small gift box, or a container with a lid. Taping the container closed will make this experience more challenging.
- Hide a surprise in a loosely knotted scarf. Have your child untie the scarf to find the object.
- Wrap a surprise in wrapping paper. Have your child unwrap the package to find the object.
- Line the edge of a metal loaf pan with old-fashioned wooden clothespins. Have your child remove the clothespins and put them in the pan.
- Wrap crayons or chalk with masking tape to resist breakage.
- Sharpen crayons by running them under hot water and shaping them with your fingers.
- Mix these ingredients together to create a finger paint that can be used indoors (preferably in the shower or tub) or outdoors:
    - 1 cup liquid laundry starch
    - 1 cup cold water
    - 3 cups soap flakes
    - 1 teaspoon tempera paint
- Make some "tunnels" by cutting the tops and bottoms out of cardboard boxes.

www.ingramcontent.com/pod-product-compliance
Lightning Source LLC
Chambersburg PA
CBHW081410070526
44583CB00020B/2754